D0583396

LEWIS and CLARK COLLEGE LIBRARY

Boards of Trustees

Boards of Trustees

Their Organization and Operation at Private Colleges and Universities

by

Henry L. Bowden

Mercer University Press

Macon, Ga. 31207

ISBN 0-86554-040-3

Copyright © 1982
Mercer University Press
Macon, GA 31207
All rights reserved.
Printed in the United States of America.

All books published by Mercer University Press are produced
on acid-free paper which exceeds the minimum standards set by the
National Historical Publications and Records Commission.

Library of Congress Cataloging in Publication Data
Bowden, Henry L., 1910-
    Boards of trustees.

    Bibliography: p. 39.
    Includes index.
    1. College trustees—Handbooks, manuals, etc.
2. Private universities and colleges—United States—
Administration—Handbooks, manuals, etc. I. Title.
LB2341.B618   1982   378′.1011   82-7991
ISBN 0-86554-040-3   AACR2

Table of Contents

Preface

ABOUT
THE
AUTHOR

For over two decades Henry L. Bowden served as the chairman of Emory University's Board of Trustees. In that capacity he dedicated his formidable talents to the welfare of Emory, with conspicuous success. During much of that time he served both as Emory's legal counsel and as Atlanta's city attorney and was invaluable in helping to tie the fortunes of the university to those of the city. In addition to a keen legal mind, he brought an innate sense of trustee responsibility to the Board and its affairs. He was ever mindful of the importance of intellectual inquiry free from all outside pressures, yet insisted that a university has its responsibilities to society as well. In recognition of his enlightened leadership in the integration of Southern colleges and universities, he was awarded, in 1963, the sixth annual Alexander Meikeljohn Award for defense of academic freedom by the American Association of University Professors. He was a key figure in the founding of the National Association of College and University Attorneys.

NACUA

In light of his rich experience as a trustee, Henry Bowden has made available this book of practical wisdom concerning the governance of colleges and universities. It should prove to be of invaluable help to all who want a more effective and involved board of trustees.

James T. Laney
President
Emory University
Atlanta, Georgia

Foreword

As Chairman of the Board of Trustees of Emory University, Henry L. Bowden had the experience, very rare for a trustee, of acquiring national media attention in 1979 when he accepted a gift to Emory from the Emily and Ernest Woodruff Fund of one hundred million dollars. That and numerous other accomplishments during his thirty-two years as a board member, twenty-two as a chairman, entitle Henry to have some opinions about how private college and university governing boards ought to organize, structure themselves, and proceed with their business. The fact that his suggestions do not in every detail exactly correspond with those of some others, including my own, only underlines one of the great basics of college trusteeship: diversity—diversity of institutions, diversity of boards, and diversity of ideas about them.

ABOUT THE AUTHOR

The lay board of trustees in higher education is a very special, almost unique, American phenomenon. It also is a very much misunderstood phenomenon. Chester L. Posey, New England advertising executive turned trustee, summarized the public perception thus:

TRUSTEES UNIQUE

> Trustees are regarded as ready-to-retire merchants on intellectual ego trips. They are often understood to receive sizable stipends to serve and almost everyone, including the faculty, believes they receive generous expense

accounts. The truth is, it can easily cost you $1,500 a year out-of-pocket to be a trustee, to say nothing of your expected donations of time and money.

TRUSTEE
"PRIVILEGES"

Veteran trustee John King says that the typical trustee "has had the privilege of being booed when introduced at football games, of being treed at board meetings by groups of enraged students; and of hiring many a new president at a salary greater than the governor's, to learn in a very short time that his institution has acquired the leadership of a dynamic windbag."

Yes, trusteeship carries its share of disappointments: it doesn't always bring appreciation; it costs something in time and money; and the public and the media are frequently negative. I sometimes wonder in the face of all the discouragements, why we have so many outstanding people volunteering for the trustee role. I am never more impressed with this fact than when I meet with the National Panel on the Distinguished Service in Trusteeship Award to sift through nominations

TRUSTEE
CONTRIBUTIONS

from scores of colleges and universities. I learn about trustees who have singlehandedly unearthed the funds to save their colleges from closing; who have provided the vision and leadership to bring academic programs into concert with a changing society; who have dealt shrewdly but compassionately with protesting students and demanding faculty; who have given hard-pressed college presidents unwavering support against community misunderstanding; and who have had the alertness to help their campuses expand when expansion was needed, and the foresight to help it contract when the boom went by.

It is true that nominees for the Distinguished Service in Trusteeship Award are by definition standouts among their peers. Yet there are far more conscientious and dedicated people on our governing boards than the popular stereotype suggests. A survey of the boards of eight private colleges in the Midwest found that the average board's total contribution to the college was 66,917 dollars, representing an average gift per trustee of over 2,000 dollars. Where trustees solicited gifts, they brought in from 2,000 to 112,000 dollars. Such *giving and getting* is what keeps most of our private colleges going, to the nation's benefit.

Such giving and getting was also at one time almost all a board of trustees was expected to do, the only other serious function assigned it being the appointment of the president. Board functions were bluntly described as "Choose the president and see that the bills are paid." And even more bluntly as "Give, get, or get off." Today boards deal with problems their predecessors of a generation or two ago would hardly have thought of touching. A recent conference of the Association of Governing Boards tackled (among other topics) federal relations, legal issues, student recruitment, international education, collective bargaining, long range planning, early faculty retirement, accreditation problems, and maintaining academic quality. John W. Nason, perhaps our leading elder statesman on trusteeship, recently expanded his classic list of Ten Trustee Responsibilities to Twelve Trustee Responsibilities: appointing the president; supporting the president; monitoring the president's performance; clarifying the institution's mission; approving long range plans; overseeing the educational program; ensuring financial solvency; preserving institutional independence; enhancing the public image; interpreting the community to the campus; serving as a court of appeal; and assessing board performance.

Does it much matter how well our volunteer trustees manage to do their many-sided jobs? Richard W. Lyman, the president of the Rockefeller Foundation and former president of Stanford University, says: "It is as much the survival of good health of the lay governing board as anything that has, so far at least, enabled the leading American private universities and colleges to avoid the fate of their European colleagues: takeover by the State." And Glenn Dumke, the chancellor of the California State Colleges, says: "America has made many contributions to higher education, but none

TRUSTEES AS BUFFERS

more important or far-reaching than the idea of having a group of interested lay citizens assume authority over the academy and act as a buffer between it and society."

The role has never been as easy as some people imagined. Many decades ago President Eliot of Harvard University commented that "the high honors of the function (of trusteeship) are in these days most

TRUSTEESHIP: HONOR AND JOY

generously earned," a sentiment Dr. Eliot would surely repeat if he were around today. Yet, trustees keep volunteering. "Being a trustee is a joy most of the time to most trustees," says John King, "because the trustee's role provides a window to the soul of the college." And Chester Posey, despite all the popular misconceptions and other negative aspects, urges, "If you get a chance to be a trustee, leap at it."

Today trustee nominating committees are seeking out a wider range of candidates for their boards than they used to, taking care to include women and members of minorities and also looking for special talents—experience in investment or money management, academic experience (an administrator or professor from another college), public relations, and even marketing. Good people, once recruited, need to be fitted into the board's organization and procedures. Henry Bowden's long experience in doing this will surely be of value to other board chairmen, presidents, and trustees.

Robert L. Gale
President
Association of Governing Boards
of Universities and Colleges

Introduction

There are all sorts of "how to" books and pamphlets. They undertake to tell us precisely how to do this or that. They give the reader the impression that the author has decided there is but a single way to do whatever is being explained. I do not wish to give such an impression. The object of this handbook is not to point out *the* way but simply to explain *one* way in which a board of trustees of a private college or university may operate successfully. This handbook is not about public institutions, though some of it may have some relevance to them.

"HOW TO" BOOKS

A "ONE WAY" HANDBOOK

The suggestions embodied in this handbook are not derived from guesswork. They have grown out of experience in the organization and operation of boards of trustees of private colleges and universities.

The treatment is not claimed to be exhaustive but touches only some common problems recognized to exist on most campuses.

NOT EXHAUSTIVE BUT REPRESENTATIVE

It is assumed that most private colleges and universities have been organized or sponsored by a specific group, whether it is a church or some other organization. That being the case, the charter or organizational papers by which such an institution was founded were prepared pursuant to the laws of the state in which the institution is located. In such papers the controlling body of the institution, whether it be a board of trustees, governors, regents, or directors, is usually set out

INSTITUTION CHARTER

in some detail—its name, its size, and the nature of its membership.

There are a number of excellent books dealing with educational governance. Some are more practical and readable than others. One of the very best that I have read is the book, *The Academic Procession,* by Henry Wriston. Wriston often was referred to as "the president's president" and his wide experience in the whole of college and university operations gives him the necessary credentials to be able to speak with authority.

RECOMMENDED
READING

Size of the Board

It has been my observation that, in general, governing boards are too large. The ideal number of members seems to be about twenty-five. If the membership is great, the members feel little distinction in being asked to join. If it is small, the work load on the few becomes so burdensome as to be oppressive. There must be a feeling on the part of the members that if they are not present for the meetings, the work of the institution will not be performed properly. Each institution should decide the appropriate number for its purposes, whether exactly twenty-five or not. If organizational papers call for a number greater or smaller than the appropriate one, these papers usually can be amended to bring the board to the proper size.

OFTEN TOO BIG

IDEAL NUMBER OF BOARD MEMBERS

Place of Residence

Often an effort is made to seek wide geographical coverage on boards in order to demonstrate that the institution is not strictly local but has a nationwide base. Such an attitude may lead to disaster. The work of the board generally will be carried on by committees, and these committees, if they work effectively, must meet with frequency on the campus of the institution. To expect members from distant points to attend such meetings is wishful thinking. Rarely will those living at

DISTANCE AND ACCESSIBILITY

a distance from the campus be regular in attendance at committee meetings. "At a distance" means about one hundred miles. Living much farther diminishes the frequency of attendance. It may be acceptable to have members from remote points, but such members are basically "show horses" and not "work horses." They should not be included as members of important committees, and especially not the executive committee.

How to Select Members

SELF–
PERPETUATION
IMPORTANT

Preferably the board should be organized as a self-perpetuating body. By that I mean that members should be elected by existing members and not "put on" the body by outside agencies of any kind. They should not come to membership on the board as representatives of any constituency other than the broad body of those who support and believe in the institution.

It must be remembered that, in general, private institutions are supported by private gifts and grants. Private colleges and universities are not entitled to ask for appropriations from state legislatures. Therefore, in selecting members of the board, keep in mind that

EXPERIENCE
AND
CAPABILITY
VITAL

the board must have experienced and capable business and professional leaders who should have the potential of either contributing to the financial support of the institution or of leading the board directly to sources of such financial support. Frequently it is said, "Why do you not put so-and-so on the board? He or she is a fine person." The fact of being a "fine person" cannot be completely discounted, but sometimes such persons simply cannot help the board get the necessary financial support and are so powerless as to be incapable of fighting their way out of a wet paper sack. The board must select recognized and effective people. Such persons will, in all probability, also be "fine persons." But the fact that they are "fine persons" cannot be the only criterion for selection.

The selection process should be carried out by a committee known as the *Committee on Nominations.* This committee should be composed of no more than five members, and they should be of varying persuasions. When board vacancies exist or are about to exist, the membership of the board should be advised of the number of such vacancies and the date of the election to fill them, and should be requested to suggest names to be considered. But that is not enough. The Committee on Nominations should canvass the field of recognized leaders in the community and seek out persons with acknowledged abilities and then seek to persuade such persons to agree to serve on the board if elected. In encouraging such persons the committee should not emphasize that membership is an honor nor should it say that little work is involved. It should be stated that the board is a working board and that work is required of the members. If unwilling to respond to such an appeal, the person should not be made a member. The honor will come from membership only as the members, by their performance, make the institution such as to command respect by the public. In ninety-nine out of one hundred cases, the persons selected by the Committee on Nominations will agree to serve, and will be approved by the full board at the proper time.

It is important that the chairman of the Committee on Nominations:

- advise the chairman of the board of trustees of the suggested nominations

- and request of the chairman of the board of trustees that he* (1) confer with prosepctive new

COMMITTEE ON NOMINATIONS

CANVASSING CANDOR

---

*Note: Wherever in this handbook I use the masculine pronoun, it is designated to extend to and include the feminine as well.

members, (2) advise them of their possible selection, (3) outline the work required, and (4) get an affirmative response, before submitting their names for action by the full board. One advantage in having the chairman of the board of trustees do this "sounding out" is that, after being elected, the person will feel some personal obligation to the board chairman to live up to what is expected and to support where possible the chairman's program.

"SOUNDING OUT" NOMINEES

STAGGERED TERMS

The terms of office of the members should be staggered so that approximately one-fifth of them come up for re-election each year. Thus, on a board of twenty-five members, five-year terms would be proper, and five members would be elected or re-elected each year.

So often little or no instructions or guidelines are given to new trustees. It is assumed that by being selected they must have demonstrated ability to handle any problem, within or without the educational field. That is just not so. It is unfair to new trustees and unfair to the institution they have agreed to serve (without compensation) to expect of new trustees that they bring to the job as trustee all of the knowledge that is needed to be effective. New trustees, and in fact those who have served for some time, should continually be urged to read new publications (and old ones they may not have read) so that they may realize that colleges and universities are not businesses and that there often are different ways to deal with their problems than those usually followed in business. A compliment will not enable one to pay the rent or ride a bus, yet there are many in educational positions who feel that a pat on the back on some occasions is even better than a raise in pay. But with this one cannot go too far, and trustees need to learn that early. One of the better guides for trustees is the book by Myron T. Wicke entitled *Handbook for Trustees*, published in 1962.

ONGOING TRUSTEE "EDUCATION"

Should Faculty or Students Be on the Board?

The answer to this question is No, and there are several reasons for that answer. One reason is that there should be no representation on the board of any special-interest groups. Faculty and students are special-interest groups. All constituent groups should be represented with equal zeal by all board members. If members represent particular groups they will feel the necessity to "go back" to their groups and lay out all that was said and done. This generally is not good. The minutes of the board of trustees meetings *should* be made available to interested persons, but in the minutes only ultimate decisions are made known and not the details of the discussions which led to such decisions.

NO SELF-INTEREST GROUPS

Another reason is that there may be a conflict of interest. When the board must take action on such matters as faculty salaries, student accommodations, student conduct, and the like, objective consideration by faculty members and students becomes difficult.

But of even greater importance is the fact that presence at the board meetings of faculty and students inhibits full and free discussions by other board members. Difficult and seemingly harsh decisions that affect faculty and students frequently must be made. These decisions may be preceded by spirited discussion. Trustees, being human, sometimes tend to make extravagant statements about academic affairs. Trustees may not wish to make critical statements in the presence of those affected, and, consequently, they may not enter into the discussion of matters affecting those present. In such circumstances, because of a continuing feeling of being inhibited, some members elect to resign.

OBJECTIVITY REQUIRED

A debate has long existed as to whether faculty and students should serve on boards of trustees. My position is clear: they should not. The schools, which I have known of and observed, that allow students and faculty to serve on their boards of trustees, would have more efficient board operations if this practice did not exist. A nationwide bluestocking committee recently was created to study the questions. The report of that committee supported the position I take here: it is not good practice to allow faculty and/or students to serve on boards of trustees.

A faculty person at one institution who resented students seeking to become involved in what he considered to be exclusively faculty concerns (such as the establishment of curricula) offered himself as a candidate for president of the student government of the institution. When the students told him he could not run because he was not a student but was a faculty member, he explained that his reason for taking such a step was that the students had sought to become members of faculty committees and that he felt to allow him to run for student-body office would be nothing short of fair play. His point was well taken, and the participation of students in faculty affairs was no longer a problem. There are some things that are the exclusive function of certain groups and no overlapping should be permitted.

No man in higher education is better qualified to deal with problems of trusteeship than John W. Nason. He recently has completed and had published a book entitled *Student-Faculty Trusteeship* which includes a short debate on this subject. John Nason and I may not agree on all points in this debate but the reading of his book is certainly recommended.

Board Meetings

The full board of trustees (or regents, or whatever) should meet at least twice annually. More frequent meetings become burdensome both to board members and to the administration of the institution, since it is the administration which must arrange the program for these meetings.

FULL
BOARD
SEMIANNUALLY

Full board meetings are basically "report meetings" to hear reports of progress by the president, reports of actions by board committees, and other reports such as those of the treasurer of the institution, deans, and other leaders. Major decisions are seldom reached or even discussed at these full board meetings. Questions should be asked and answered, information should be relayed, and institutional goals and purposes should be discussed.

"REPORT
MEETINGS"

Further, I strongly recommend having a dinner once a year the night before one of the meetings of the full board, a dinner attended by the members, wives or husbands, and the principal educational officers and administrative leaders of the institution. You will need a good speaker, either from within or without the institution. If you are careful to get good speakers, the dinner meetings will be well attended and looked forward to; if not, you may find it hard to get a representative crowd the second year.

GETTING
ACQUAINTED
MEALS

Concerning the formal gathering the next day, three basic elements go into the conduct of a good board meeting. First, there must be something of substance about which to meet. Do not meet just to be meeting. Second, do not waste time. The members' time is valuable. Get the business of the meeting accomplished with dispatch but without any seeming hurry or glossing over of important business. Third, have a good time around

MEETINGS
SERIOUS
AND OPEN

the board table. Encourage banter between and among the committee members. Encourage the swapping of stories, the asking of questions, and other such exchanges. This makes for a lively session and one which most trustees will enjoy and look forward to.

The Committee System

The traditional organization of the board into committees, which are responsible for certain of the board's several areas of concern, is effective and desirable. First of all, there should be an *Executive Committee* with broad membership, usually composed of about half of the members of the board. In addition, there should be, at the least, the following committees: committees on Academic Affairs, Budget, Buildings and Grounds, Development, Investment, Nominations, Real Estate, and Student Affairs. There may be such other committees as the particular personality of the institution may dictate. The chairman should be authorized to establish *ad hoc* committees as he may deem necessary.

KINDS OF COMMITTEES NEEDED

Matters falling within the function of each committee should be referred promptly to it for action and for a report to the board or to the executive committee. This is important, for if the chairman fails so to assign work responsibility and assumes such functions himself, the committees will soon lose interest. Assigning work to board members and calling on them for decisions and reports creates a feeling of contributing and makes a member feel more keenly his own importance in the whole governance function.

COMMITTEES NEED WORK TO DO

The Executive Committee

Though a board of trustees usually has the responsibility of deciding questions of policy in connection with the operation of the institution, the full board must meet so infrequently that it is important to delegate complete authority between meetings to the Executive Committee. This is why the Executive Committee should be made up of a relatively large number of trustees. The Executive Committee should meet at a fixed time every month, including the summer months. The chairman of the board also should be the chairman of the Executive Committee. The decisions of the Executive Committee should carry the weight of full board decisions. The Executive Committee's meetings should take place on campus.

THE EXECUTIVE EXECUTES

Only Executive Committee members, the president of the institution, and such other persons as may be agreed upon jointly by the president and the chairman of the board should attend. Usually the president will wish to have his principal administrative officers and possibly one or two others there. Confidentiality and secrecy as to proceedings should be impressed on those in attendance. Full minutes of the meetings should be sent to all members of the board as promptly after conclusion of the meetings as possible. The minutes usually are prepared by the secretary of the institution and submitted to the president and the chairman to check for accuracy before being circulated.

CONFIDEN-TIALITY AND MINUTES

Each meeting of the executive committee should be preceded by a luncheon for the members and other invited guests. It is a good practice to invite to the luncheon portion faculty members and students in small numbers each month so they may observe what goes on, and so the members of the board may get to know them. It also is a good practice to invite to the luncheon portion once a year representatives of the local governing authorities such as the city council, county manager, or county commissioner. This tends to break down the too-frequent separation of campus from community—

LUNCHEON TO BOLSTER UNDERSTANDING

sometimes referred to as Town and Gown.

Other Committees

ACADEMIC
AFFAIRS
COMMITTEE

To the *Academic Affairs Committee* should be referred all matters having to do with approval of curriculum changes, the award of honorary degrees, and the extension of tenure to faculty persons. The board should be able to know what the committee feels about the propriety of extending tenure in every case. The faculty and the president usually must first recommend tenure grants, and it is hardly thinkable that the board would turn down such a recommendation, but the board, at least, ought to know that one of its own committees has looked at the matter and has also approved it.

The Academic Affairs Committee will find it useful, at least twice a year, at the expense of the institution, to meet for dinner at some convenient place off campus with, say, eight members of the faculty. These faculty members should be different ones each time and should be selected by the dean of faculties or the dean of the

FACULTY
INPUT

school from which they come. A wide diversity of faculty persons should be selected each time so they may not only meet the members of the board, but also know one another better, since faculty members in one division or school may have little chance to get to know their counterparts in others. At these meetings the trustees should try to bring up for discussion any and all things in connection with the institution which the faculty wishes to discuss, with the exception of salaries of individual faculty members, since these matters are too personal to be discussed in such an open meeting. It is good for the chairman of the board of trustees, if at all possible, to attend these meetings and to get to know the faculty people and let them see that the chairman is not the ogre that someone possibly has described him as being. It also enables the trustees to learn, sometimes to their surprise, that faculty persons can be normal, likeable people too, with attitudes and persuasions much similar to those of the trustees.

The *Budget Committee* examines with great care the proposed budget as recommended to it by the president after he has conducted budget hearings. The Budget Committee then gives full support to the final budget proposal at the board meeting with such modifications as the president and the committee have agreed upon. It is the budget committee that also must annually fix the salary of the president and the other major administrative officers to make certain that good work is rewarded with appropriate increases in compensation.

BUDGET COMMITTEE

The *Buildings and Grounds Committee* should establish an overall plan for campus use in order to assure the preservation of campus appearance, the maximum utilization of campus space, the acquisition of additional real estate as it may become available adjacent to the campus, and the location of new buildings and other installations. Remodeling, demolition, maintenance, and repair of all campus properties should also come within the general supervision of this committee.

BUILDINGS AND GROUNDS COMMITTEE

In all colleges and universities the need for continued support is a concern of major importance. Thus, a continuing program of development of facilities is not only desirable but necessary. The *Development Committee* determines when special fund-raising efforts are to be undertaken, serves as the principal guiding agency of the development office of the institution, and determines priorities among the ever-increasing needs of the institution.

DEVELOPMENT COMMITTEE

The *Investment Committee* oversees the investment of the college or university's funds. This is usually handled through some established banking institution

INVESTMENT COMMITTEE

with which the committee works closely. Continued support of an institution is encouraged by the care and productivity of that which has previously been given, as demonstrated by the board of trustees. Careless handling of what has been given does not recommend further gifts. Therefore, the work of this committee is of major importance. The committee should have from five to seven members. Since purchases and sales must in some instances be made with dispatch, it is good for the bylaws of the institution to provide that the concurrence of any three members of the committee in a purchase or sale will suffice. Full reports of all purchases and sales should be reported promptly to the executive committee and included in its regular monthly minutes.

COMMITTEE ON NOMINATIONS

The *Committee on Nominations* not only should nominate new members of the board, as previously discussed (see above, pp. 3-4), but also should annually nominate the officers of the board and the members of the executive committee.

REAL ESTATE COMMITTEE

Most institutions acquire real estate remote from the campus by gift or inheritance. The *Real Estate Committee* should oversee the use of that real estate, recommend its retention or sale, and approve rental rates as applied to such properties.

COMMITTEE ON STUDENT AFFAIRS

Of increasing importance these days is the *Committee on Student Affairs.* Colleges and universities no longer operate *in loco parentis* as was the case a generation ago. Students today are less passive and more interested in all that goes on in the institution they are attending. They wish to be kept informed, even though they may not be involved in the actual governance. The Committe on Student Affairs should hold regular off-campus meetings at least once each quarter or semester with representative students selected by the student government groups. At these gatherings, matters of general interest to students should be discussed. Housing, food, curriculum, institutional goals, athletic programs, and rules of social conduct are all proper subjects for this committee to discuss with the students. Frank and open inquiry into these things together with explanations of institutional plans and limitations, will pay off in increased confidence by the students in their alma mater.

Committees should consist of approximately five members. They should meet on the call of the committee chairman or meet with the president if he feels the need of advice from a committee. A quorum should consist of three members. **NUMBER OF MEMBERS AND QUORUM**

Ad hoc committees may be of such size as the chairman of the board shall determine and should meet as required. Committees need not meet on campus but may wish to do so, in which event adequate facilities for such meetings should be provided.

The Board and the President

Of utmost importance is a closeness between the chairman of the board of trustees and the president of the institution. For the two of them to meet together for coffee or lunch at least once a week is most desirable, where possible. The chairman of the board should be kept informed about what is happening on the campus and the president should know of community attitudes and feelings. Such closeness pays great dividends. **THE CHAIRMAN AND THE PRESIDENT**

The usual approach to governance of educational institutionals is for the board of trustees to enunciate broad policy and for the president and his staff to make all administrative decisions. **APPROACH TO GOVERNANCE**

Frequently there is a question whether a given matter requires a policy decision or an administrative decision. Whenever possible such matters should be declared to **DECISIONS: POLICY OR ADMINISTRATIVE** be administrative decisions rather than policy decisions. The board of trustees should be extremely careful not to invade the administrative decision-making authority of the president. Most presidents take pride in their abilities to handle campus problems effectively. They are far better acquainted with campus feelings and passions than are the members of the board. If the board frequently invades these rights of the president, the president is likely to resign, and properly so. On the other hand, the president, in making such decisions, will very often outline the problem to the board chairman or other members of the board and seek their counsel and help in arriving at proper administrative conclusions.

Where basic policies are *demanded*, not only should the board face up to its responsibilities to act, but the president will wish for the board to act in order to give him the guidance and direction that he needs in such matters. A wise board, however, seeks the advice of the president in arriving at such basic policy decisions.

Taking Stock

PERIODIC
INVENTORY

Approximately every five years the entire board of trustees should hold a meeting at some resort-type place, a meeting that includes not only business sessions but ample time for recreation such as golf, swimming, tennis, and other pleasurable activities. The event should be paid for entirely by the institution, should include the husbands and wives of the members, and should last two to three days. It will enable the members of the board to take inventory of institutional assets, reexamine institutional goals, and get to know the families of other members.

The president and such other institutional officials as he and the chairman may agree upon should also attend this occasional meeting. To have some individual who has wide experience in the field of education, finance, or administration address the assemblage can be helpful. If the husbands and wives of the board members are invited to all sessions, including the business sessions, this will serve to educate them as to the nature of the work being performed by their spouses and make them more tolerant and indulgent when it seems that the institution makes undue demands on the spouses' time.

INVOLVING MEMBERS' FAMILIES

Such gatherings are sometimes called "retreats." To hold them frequently serves no good purpose. To hold them every five or six years is of great help to the institution. At least one institution felt that the word "retreat" carried connotations of defeat and it elected to call the meeting an "attack" rather than a retreat, since in actuality the board would be attacking the problems of the institution and seeking to decide them affirmatively rather than to be retreating from those problems as if they were too great to be dealt with.

"ATTACK"

In addition to this sort of meeting, there are others which board members may attend with profit. I want to mention especially the meetings of the Association of Governing Boards of Colleges and Universities. This organization has a membership that is broadly representative of the nation's system of higher education. It meets frequently and in various parts of the country, presents programs directed at real issues and not imagined ones, and all in all is well worth the attendance of as many board members as possible. Board members not only will hear experts express themselves on specific problems but also will meet members of other boards and swap experiences and gain information. The institution should pay the cost of attendance at these meetings of at least two or three of its board members each year. This will be of tremendous benefit to the institution in the long run.

AGB MEETINGS

Increasingly, members of boards of trustees of elee-

MEMBER
INDEMNITY

mosynary institutions in general have been subjected to law suits over matters which a decade ago would never have been sanctioned by the courts. Liability of such trustees in many cases has been declared to exist and monetary judgments obtained. The institution should indemnify its board members against loss growing out of such suits. Included in the suggested bylaws appended hereto is a statement on that subject, suggesting one good way to deal with it.

The Charter

THE
RIGHT
WORDS

The legal document by which an incorporated institution comes into being is variously known as a charter, constitution, or some other appropriate title. The proper wording of that document is of extreme importance. It is from the expressions of such a document that the powers and authorities of the institution are broadly determined. Thus, if the document fails to enunciate a right, that right does not usually exist unless the state sets it forth by statute.

OUTLINE
OF POWERS

To make the powers as broad as possible is of considerable solace to the board of trustees and the administration when innovative programs are being considered. Unless the right to engage in an activity is approved by the charter, the institution generally cannot engage in it. Below, in rather legal language, is a statement of powers which will suffice to cover almost any area in which an educational institution may wish to become involved. I suggest that the provisions of one's own institution's charter be reexamined and, if its powers are not sufficiently broad, that it be amended so as to include these suggested powers.

TO ACQUIRE
PROPERTY

§ The corporation shall have power to acquire both real and personal property by purchase, exchange, devise, gift, or donation, and to hold, use, or invest same in such way and manner as may tend to promote the objects of said corporation; and to carry out all trusts imposed by the donors, including especially the right, without any order of court, to lend on security approved by it, or to otherwise invest any and all funds which may be received by it as endowment. Provided, however, that all property, real or personal, that may be purchased or otherwise acquired by said corporation, shall be received and held in trust, that it shall be used, kept, maintained, and disposed of for the educational purposes in this charter set forth. Petitioners also desire for said corporation the power to have a common seal, to sue and be sued under the corporate name above stated; to keep and maintain order and discipline among its student body, and on its campus; to make any and all contracts with reference to acquisition, management, control, incumbrance, sale, or disposition of its property not contrary to the laws of this state, or of the United States.

§ Said corporation shall also have authority to give or provide for instruction in theology and all of the arts, sciences and professions, and in all branches of higher instruction and learning, and to that end to establish or acquire such schools, departments and faculties as it may deem proper; and in connection with the medical school established or maintained by it, to establish or acquire and maintain such hospital, dispensary, and training school of nurses as may be necessary or useful in connection therewith.

TO PROVIDE
INSTRUCTION

TO
CONSOLIDATE
OR AFFILIATE

§ Said corporation shall also have power and authority to receive by donation or purchase or to otherwise acquire, upon such terms as may be agreed upon, either by way of merger or consolidation, the property assets and good will of any other college, school, or institution of learning, or to become affiliated therewith upon such terms and conditions and to such extent and for such purposes as may be agreed upon, or to receive, maintain, support and control any such college or institution as a department of such university, with power to appoint or elect the trustees thereof, if the same is maintained as a separate corporation; or to agree with any other such college or institution as to basis of correlation of departments, of courses of study or any other means by which the work thereof may be correlated with the work of said university.

§ Also, power and authority to prescribe the course of study and the degrees of proficiency therein necessary to graduation in any school or department, or under any faculty created, maintained or controlled by it, and to grant such diplomas or certificates to graduates or students in any of such schools or departments, or affiliated colleges, or under any such faculty as it may deem proper, and to confer such degrees upon such graduates as may be appropriate, and such as are conferred by other universities maintaining or controlling similar schools of instruction and learning; also to grant honorary degrees to persons distinguished for learning, ability, and character in their respective vocations.

TO CONFER
DEGREES

§ Said corporation shall also have power to make and adopt all such bylaws, rules, and regulations as may seem to be necessary or proper for the management, control, and conduct of the affairs and property of said university, and said bylaws, rules, and regulations so adopted shall be binding on said corporation until amended in the manner and form prescribed therein for their amendment; provided, none of said bylaws, rules, or regulations shall be contrary to any of the laws of this state or of the United States; and said corporation shall also have all other such powers or authority as are usually or properly conferred upon or possessed by universities or similiar institutions for higher learning elsewhere.

TO
LEGISLATE

The Bylaws

As adjuncts to the basic charter, the institution should adopt a full and exhaustive set of bylaws. These stand at a secondary level to the charter just as federal laws do to the United States Constitution, but, in many instances, they are even more important than the charter since they govern the day-to-day operations of the institution. Bylaws will, of course, vary with each institution. Below are some suggested bylaw provisions which certainly will bear careful examination for possible inclusion in those of any institution. This list does not attempt to be exhaustive, but only to suggest some provisions of a general nature that can be of great value to a board of trustees.

BYLAWS AND
DAY-TO-DAY
OPERATIONS

Bylaws about Meetings

The following suggested provisions apply to board meetings:

§ *Special Meetings.* The chairman of the board of trustees may at any time call a special meeting of the board of trustees if he judge it

CALLED
MEETINGS

necessary, and he *shall* call a special meeting of the board on the written request of five members. In case of the death, absence, or disability of the chairman of the board, the calling of special meetings shall be the duty of the vice-chairman.

QUORUM

§ *Quorum.* Fifteen members shall constitute a quorum for the transaction of business in any meeting of the full board. A smaller number may adjourn from time to time until a quorum is obtained.

ABSENCES

§ *Absence.* Any member of the board of trustees who is absent from two consecutive annual meetings without being excused by a majority vote of those present at the meetings from which he is absent shall be dropped from membership on the board unless he shall elect, after being given the opportunity in writing to do so, to become a trustee-emeritus, provided he is eligible for such position.

EMERITUS
MEMBERS

§ *Trustees-Emeriti.* Any member of the board of trustees who has served as much as one full term of five years may be elected by the board as a Trustee-Emeritus. Any member of the board of trustees who attains the age of seventy (70) years shall, effective with the end of the annual meeting of the board of trustees following his attainment of such age, become a

Trustee-Emeritus.

A Trustee-Emeritus shall be entitled to attend and shall receive notices of all meetings of the full board of trustees and shall have every privilege of regular membership on the board except that of voting, but shall not be counted in determining the number of trustees permitted by the charter or in determining whether a quorum is present. The secretary shall notify, in writing, persons who have become Trustees-Emeriti.

EMERITUS
PRIVILEGES

§ *Notice.* Written notice of the time and place of all meetings of the board of trustees, regular or special, shall be sent to each trustee at least ten days before the date of the meeting.

NOTICE OF
MEETINGS

§ *Agenda.* Any business may be transacted at any meeting of the board of trustees. The purposes for which special meetings are called may be, but shall not necessarily be, set forth in the notice of the special meeting sent to the members.

AGENDA

It is good to make way for younger persons to become members of the board of trustees but it is also good to hold on to the counsel and advice which can come only from older heads. Hence the provision for retirement from the board at age seventy as well as the retention of the member in an emeritus status.

EXPERIENCE
COUNTS

Officers of the Board

The following bylaw suggestions deal with the officers of the board of trustees:

§ *Officers.* The regular officers of the board shall consist of a Chairman, a Vice-Chairman, and a Secretary. They shall be elected annually

OFFICERS
NEEDED

from among the board's membership and shall continue in office for one year or until their successors are named. Any officer of the board may be removed from office at the will of the board at any time.

CHAIRMAN

§ *The Chairman.* The Chairman shall call to order and preside at all meetings of the board, and, as the authoritative head of the board, shall represent the board at the public meetings of the institution.

The Chairman shall be an ex-officio member of all standing and special committees, with the right to vote, but he shall not be counted in determining the presence of a quorum at meetings of committees. Unless otherwise provided in these bylaws, the Chairman shall also have the power to designate any member or members

DUTIES

of the board of trustees of his own selection to represent the institution at public meetings or other meetings, and to perform other functions of the Chairman in the event for any reason the vice-chairman is not available. The Chairman shall also vote all proxies and represent the institution at corporate meetings of companies in which the institution has a financial interest. In the absence or disability of the Chairman and the vice-chairman, the chairman of the investment committee shall so represent the institution at such corporate meetings.

VICE-CHAIRMAN

§ *The Vice-Chairman.* The Vice-Chairman shall perform the duties of the chairman in the event of the absence or disability of the chairman.

SECRETARY

§ *The Secretary.* The Secretary shall record and preserve the minutes of the meetings of the board of trustees and its executive committee.

He shall affix the seal and attest as may be required for the transaction of the institution's business. The board of trustees may, if it desires, elect an Assistant Secretary, who need not be a member of the board and who shall be empowered to exercise all the duties of the Secretary in the absence of the Secretary.

§ *Official Signatures.* All official papers, documents, contracts, and other written instruments necessary to carry on the administration of the affairs of the institution or the work of the board of trustees shall be signed by the chairman of the board of trustees or the president of the institution or by such other person or persons as may from time to time be directed by the executive committee.

OFFICIAL
SIGNATURES

Officers of the Institution

The president generally likes to have his duties spelled out. He is entitled to such a statement in order that he will know what is expected of him. The following suggested bylaws deal with the president and the chancellor (usually a retired president):

§ *The President.* There shall be a President of the institution who shall be elected by the board of trustees, to serve at the pleasure of the board. The President shall be the chief executive and administrative officer, responsible to, and reporting directly to, the board of trustees. He shall be charged with the duty of supervising all the interests of the university with the aid of the faculty and the administrative staff. He shall establish, with the approval of the board of trustees or its executive committee, such admi-

PRESIDENT

CHIEF
EXECUTIVE

nistrative offices and faculty positions as he may deem necessary for carrying on the work of the institution. He shall nominate for approval by the board of trustees or its executive committee all principal executive officers and all faculty members recommended for continuous appointment.

REPRESENTS THE INSTITUTION

The President shall represent the institution on public occasions connected with the operation of the institution and shall confer all properly authorized degrees. It shall be his duty to organize the faculties of the institution and of the several divisions, schools, or colleges, direct the methods of their meetings, and supervise their work. He is charged particularly with responsibility for the internal order and discipline of the institution, and to this end he shall hold all deans and members of the faculty to the faithful and efficient discharge of their duties. He may, when he deems it advisable, preside over any meetings of the faculties.

MEETS WITH TRUSTEES

As the chief administrative officer, the President shall attend all meetings of the board of trustees and of its executive committee, and he may, at his discretion, attend meetings of other committees of the board, and participate in their discussions.

REPORTS TO TRUSTEES

He shall cause accurate reports of the fiscal and other affairs to be prepared and submitted to the board of trustees. It shall be his duty to bring to the attention of the board of trustees all matters within his knowledge that in his opinion affect the interest of the institution and require consideration by the board.

IN THE PRESIDENT'S ABSENCE

In case of the death or extended absence or disability of the president, the executive vice-president (or such other second-in-command that the institution may have) shall serve as Acting President. In case the office of executive vice-president has not been filled, the board of trustees or its executive committee shall as promptly as possible designate an acting president to serve until a president shall have been elected and shall have assumed office. On the death of the president, an acting president, although charged with performing the duties of the president, will not automatically succeed to the presidency.

§ *The Chancellor.* The board of trustees may, in its discretion, elect a Chancellor. The Chancellor shall have general advisory relationship to the adminstration but shall not be charged with administrative duties. He shall have the right to attend meetings of the board of trustees and of its executive committee and to participate in their discussions, but without vote. He may, in his discretion, attend meetings of the faculty and senate, if any, and participate in their discussions. He shall counsel with the president on matters of administrative policy and on any matters affecting the interest and work of the institution and may, within his discretion, render such other service to the institution as may be requested by the president or the board of trustees.

CHANCELLOR:

ADVISOR AND COUNSELLOR

Bylaws about the Faculty

Lines of authority in carrying out the instructional program of the institution are jealously regarded by faculty persons. Therefore, the suggested bylaws which

LINES OF AUTHORITY

follow should be considered in order that these lines of authority may be clear:

§ *Faculty*. Responsibility for the instructional programs shall be vested in the faculty under the direction of the president. The faculty shall include the president, the vice-presidents, deans, professors, associate professors, instructors, and persons of such other rank or title as the president may recommend.

FACULTY MEMBERSHIP

The faculty of any division, school, or college shall include all such officers as have responsibility for instruction in that division, school, or college. A member of the faculty may be a member of the faculty of more than one division, school, or college.

Subject to general institutional policy and regulations and to the powers vested in the president and the faculty senate, the faculty of any division, school, or college shall have jurisdiction over the educational program and the internal affairs of that division, school, or college including such matters as admission requirements, curricula, instruction, schedules, and degree requirements.

FACULTY JURISDICTION

§ *Deans*. The Dean of a school or college shall be appointed by the board of trustees or its executive committee upon recommendation of the president, who shall have conferred regarding such recommendation with an appropriate committee of the members of the faculty of the school or college. The president shall also report to the board a vote taken by the faculty of the school concerned on the person recommended. The Dean of a school or college shall have general responsibility for the direction of the

DEANS

SELECTION

DUTIES

work of his area of responsibility and shall be responsible to the president for the administration thereof. He shall exercise leadership in the development of educational policies and programs. He shall preside at meetings of the faculty of his school or college except when the president chooses to preside; he shall supervise the work and direct the discipline of his division; he shall advise with the president in the formation of the faculty, the determination of curricula, and concerning all the interests of his school or college, including its relationships to other divisions of the institution and to the interests of the institution as a whole.

§ *Faculty Appointments.* Appointments to membership on the faculty, other than the president, vice-presidents, and deans shall be of two kinds—limited and continuous. A limited appointment is one which is terminated at the close of a period of time specified in writing to the appointee. A continuous appointment is one which will not be terminated by the institution except for adequate cause as specified in the principles approved and published by the board of trustees, or by retirement in accordance with the provisions of the institution's retirement plan.

FACULTY APPOINTMENTS:

Limited appointments shall be made by the president upon recommendation of the dean of the school or college primarily concerned and shall be reported to the board of trustees or its executive committee.

LIMITED

Continous appointments shall be made by the board of trustees or its executive committee upon the recommendation of the president who

CONTINUOUS

shall have conferred regarding such recommendation with the dean of the school or college primarily concerned.

Each dean shall establish and communicate to his faculty the procedures for expressing faculty opinion in matters of individual appointment, promotion, and termination. The precise terms and conditions of each appointment shall be stated in writing, shall be in accordance with the principles approved and published by the board of trustees, and shall be in possession both of the institution and the appointee before the appointment is final.

TERMS AND CONDITIONS

Conflict of Interest

CONFLICT OF INTEREST BYLAW

Given the broad areas of business and professional activities engaged in by members of the board, it is not unusual that there could exist some degree of conflict of interest. The suggested bylaw which is set out below is designated to clarify the duty of each trustee to meet such problems in a direct manner:

The following conflict of interest policy is hereby adopted:

Any duality of interest or possible conflict of interest on the part of any trustee or administrative official or employee of the institution should be disclosed to the president of the institution, chairman of the board of trustees, and through the chairman to the executive committee and made a matter of record, either through an annual procedure or when the interest becomes a matter of administrative or trustee action.

RESPONSIBILITY FOR DISCLOSURE

Any such trustee, officer, administrative official, or employee having a duality of interest or possible conflict of interest on any matter should not vote, act, or use his personal influence on the matter, and in the case of a trustee, he should not be counted in determining a quorum for action on the issue as to which a conflict may exist, even where permitted by law, and in the case of an officer, administrative official or employee, should not determine or take action on such matter. In the case of a trustee, the minutes of a meeting involving such vote should reflect the making of the disclosure, the abstention from voting, and the quorum situation. In the case of an officer, administrative official or employee, appropriate record should be made to show that such disclosure of duality of interest was made and that he abstained from taking such action.

DUALITY OF INTEREST AND ABSTENTION

The foregoing requirements should not be construed as preventing the trustee, officer, or administrative official or employee from briefly stating in a non-argumentative manner his position in the matter or from answering pertinent questions since his knowledge may be of great assistance.

DUAL INTEREST AND "RESOURCE PERSON"

The chairman is authorized and directed to see that the foregoing policy is effectuated.

Personal Liability

Propertied persons are becoming increasingly reluctant and hesitant about becoming members, not only of corporate boards of directors, but also of boards of trustees of educational and charitable institutions. This is so because of the plethora of law suits, justified or not, which have recently been given wide publicity. In a recent case, for example, the board of a charity hospital

TRUSTEE LIABILITY

had a judgment rendered against it because of investment irregularities. These suits, in many instances, name as defendants the individual members of boards of trustees.

As a result, educational institutions are increasingly concerned, and in order to assure existing and prospective board members that they will not unnecessarily be exposed to large judgments against them, there has sprung up a custom of indemnifying board members against financial loss resulting from such suits. To fund such possible liability, educational and other charitable institutions have come to the point not only of stating such indemnification attitudes in their official bylaws but have begun taking out insurance policies to cover such.

TRUSTEE
INDEMNITY

I have set out below a suggested set of bylaws to meet such a problem. This is but one approach but it is, at least, direct and should be reassuring to prospective as well as existing board members:

TRUSTEE
INDEMNITY
BYLAW

§ Be it, therefore, prescribed that the institution shall indemnify and hold harmless any person who was or is a party or is threatened to be made a party of any threatened, pending or completed action, suit or proceeding, whether civil, criminal, administrative, or investigative (other than an action by or in the right of the institution) by reason of the fact that he is or was a trustee, officer, employee, or agent of the institution, or is or was serving at the request of the institution, as a trustee, director, officer, employee or agent of another corporation, partnership, joint venture, trust or other enterprise, against expenses (including attorneys' fees), judgments, fines, and amounts paid in settlement actually and reasonably incurred by him in connection with such action, suit or proceeding, if he acted in a manner reasonably believed to be in or not opposed to the best interests of the institution, and, with respect to any criminal action or proceeding, had no reasonable cause to believe his conduct was unlawful. The termination of any action, suit, or proceedings by judgment, order, settlement, conviction or upon a plea of "nolo contendere" or its equivalent, shall not, of itself, create a presumption that the person did not act in a manner which he reasonably believed to be in or not opposed to the best interests of the institution, and with respect to any criminal action or proceeding, had no reasonable cause to believe that his conduct was unlawful.

"BEST INTERESTS"

§ The institution shall indemnify and hold harmless any person who was or is a party or is threatened to be made a party to any threatened, pending, or completed action or proceeding by or in the right of the institution to procure a judgment in its favor by reason of the fact he is or was a trustee, officer, employee, or agent of the institution or is or was serving at the request of the university, as a trustee, director, officer, employee, or agent of another corporation, partnership, joint venture, trust, or other enterprise, against expenses (including attorneys' fees) actually and reasonably incurred by him in connection with the defense or settlement of such action or suit, if he acted in good faith and in a manner he reasonably believed to be in or not opposed to the best interests of the institution except that no indemnification shall be made in respect of any claim, issue, or matter as to which such person shall have been adjudged

"GOOD FAITH"

to be liable for negligence or misconduct in the performance of his duty to the institution, unless and only to the extent that the court in which such action or suit was brought shall determine upon application that, despite the adjudication of liability but in view of all the circumstances of the case, such person is fairly and reasonably entitled to indemnity for such expenses which the court shall deem proper.

§ To the extent that a trustee, director, officer, employee, or agent has been successful on the merits or otherwise in defense of any action, suit, or proceeding referred to or in

INDEMNITY AGAINST EXPENSES

defense of any claim, issue, or matter therein, he shall be indemnified against expenses (including attorneys' fees) actually and reasonably incurred by him in connection therewith.

§ Except herein as provided and except as may be ordered by a court, any indemnification shall be made by the institution only as authorized in the specific case upon a determination that indemnification of the trustee, director, officer, employee, or agent is proper in the

"PROPER CIRCUMSTANCES"

circumstances because he has met the applicable standards of conduct set forth. Such determination shall be made (1) by the board of trustees by a majority vote of a quorum consisting of trustees who were not parties to such action, suit, or proceeding, or (2) if such a quorum is not obtainable, or, even if obtainable, if a quorum of disinterested trustees so directs, by the firm of independent legal counsel then employed by the institution in a written opinion.

§ Expenses incurred in defending a civil or criminal action, suit, or proceeding may be paid by the institution in advance of the final disposition of such action, suit, or preceeding as authorized by the board of trustees in the specific case upon receipt of an undertaking by or on behalf of the trustee, director, officer, employee, or agent to repay such amount unless it shall ultimately be determined that he is entitled to be indemnified by the institution as authorized.

§ The indemnification provided herein shall not be deemed exclusive of any other right to which the persons indemnified hereunder shall be entitled and shall inure to the benefit of the heirs, executors, or administrators of such persons.

§ The institution may purchase and maintain insurance on behalf of any person who is or was a trustee, officer, employee, or agent, or is or was serving at the request of the institution as a trustee, director, officer, employee, or agent of another corporation, partnership, joint venture, trust, or other enterprise, against any liability asserted against him and incurred by him in any such capacity, or arising out of his status as such, whether or not the institution would have the power to indemnify him against such liability hereunder.

§ If any expenses or other amounts are paid by way of indemnification, otherwise than by court order or by an insurance carrier pursuant to insurance maintained by the institution, the institution shall, within fifteen months from the date of such payment, send by first class mail to the members of the board of trustees of the institution a statement specifying the persons paid, the amounts paid, and the nature and

AUTHORIZED
INDEMNIFICATION

INDEMNITY
INSURANCE

NOTIFICATION
OF
LITIGATION

status at the time of such payment of the litigation or threatened litigation.

Statement of Policy
on Student Relationships

POLICY
STATEMENTS:
BOARD
RESPONSIBILITY

As has been earlier stated, the traditional role of boards of colleges and universities in the United States is to determine policy, leaving to the administration the function of effectuating such policies and conducting the day-to-day affairs of the institution. In addition to the founding documents there is an established set of bylaws adopted by the board of trustees and amended from time to time. These two basic documents are general in nature.

Policy on specific matters is established by the board of trustees from time to time, and such policy is not contained in any one specific policy document.

A suggested statement of policy dealing with faculty relationships, appears above (pp. 25-28). Following is a suggested statement concerning student relationships:

STUDENT
RELATIONSHIPS
POLICY

The board of trustees hereby adopts and publishes the following statement of policy dealing with student relationships:

§ This institution was founded as, and proudly continues in its role as, an agency dedicated to seeking and imparting truth.

ADMISSION

§ Admission is open to applicants who are able to meet admission standards, regardless of race, creed, color, or place of origin; persons are not to be admitted to any of its divisions or schools by any quota or any formula based on race, creed, color, or place of origin.

ATTENDANCE
PRIVILEGE

§ Attendance is a privilege and not a right. Students applying for admission do so voluntarily and are free to withdraw at their pleasure, subject only to the fulfillment of their financial obligations to the institution.

§ By applying for admission and being accepted, each student agrees to be bound by the rules, policies, procedures, and adminstrative regulations as they exist at the time of his admission and as they may be changed, modified, or added to during the time he is a student.

STUDENT RESPONSIBILITIES AND RIGHTS

§ By admission as a student, a person acquires the right to pursue the course of study to which he is admitted, under applicable policies, rules, and procedures.

§ Students will be provided the opportunity to participate in the development of rules and procedures pertaining to student affairs to the extent that such participation and the results thereof, as determined by the board of trustees or its designated agent, are consistent with orderly processes and with the policies and administrative responsibilities of the board of trustees and the administration.

RULES CONCERNING STUDENT AFFAIRS

§ Each student is expected to conduct himself with dignity and with due respect for the rights of others, realizing that sobriety and morality are not only characteristics of a mature and responsible person but are essential to the maintenance of a free and orderly society.

STUDENT CONDUCT

§ Membership in and rules governing admission to student organizations shall be determined by the organizations themselves, and such rules shall not be required to be uniform so long as the same do not contravene any policy established by the board of trustees.

STUDENT ORGANIZATIONS

Policy Concerning Dissent and Demonstrations

The following statement of policy is suggested:

This is an educational institution; it is not a vehicle for political or social action. It appreciates and endorses the fundamental right of dissent, and fully protects and encourages the fair and reasonable exercise of this right by individuals. Because the right of dissent is subject to abuse, the board of trustees and the president publish this statement to make clear policy concerning such abuse:

GENERAL STATEMENT

§ Individuals associated with this institution represent a wide variety of viewpoints and attitudes; the school fosters the free expression and interchange of differing views through oral and written discourse and logical persuasion.

FREE EXPRESSION

§ Dissent, to be acceptable, must be orderly and peaceful, and represent constructive alternatives reasonably presented.

ORDERLY DISSENT

§ Coercion, threats, demands, obscenity, vulgarity, obstructionism, and violence are not acceptable.

DISORDERLY DISSENT

§ Demonstrations, marches, sit-ins, or noisy protests which are designed or intended to or which do disrupt normal academic and institutional pursuits will not be permitted.

DISRUPTIVE DISSENT

§ Classes and routine operations will not be suspended except for reasonable cause as determined under authority of the University President.

ABIDING BY STANDARDS

§ Administrators, faculty, other employees, and students are expected to abide by these standards of conduct in promoting their views, particularly dissent.

§ Persons who are not so inclined should not attend nor become associated with the institution, nor continue to be associated with it.

DISSOCIATION

§ Academic and administrative procedures will protect individuals in their right of free expression, and provide for prompt and appropriate disciplinary action against those who abuse such right.

PROTECTION
AND
DISCIPLINE

Conclusion

There are hundreds of private colleges and universities in this country. Most of them are relatively well managed and have capable and efficient boards of trustees. However, there is a sizable number which could improve their effectiveness in higher education by improving the organization and operation of their boards of trustees. In the past two years I have seen two private colleges change direction and accomplishment in a greatly improved way by changing the manner in which their boards of trustees operate.

INSTITUTIONAL
EFFICIENCY
DETERMINED
BY THE BOARD

It is in the interest of all private colleges and universities, despite a feeling that they are doing well, to examine their own operations critically and as objectively as possible that by such self-study they may be able continually to upgrade and improve their accomplishments in the field of higher education, which field they seek to serve.

SELF-STUDY
BEGETS
IMPROVEMENT

The point at which the most immediate improvement can be accomplished is by reducing the number of trustees. Another is to assign specific tasks to committees, and to demand that the task be handled by the committee, and that a report be made at a stated time to the full board or executive committee. Too often this

STEPS
TOWARD
IMPROVEMENT

type of task is handled by the chairman or by the administration, making the board member feel he is window dressing in contrast to being a person who is really contributing to the work of the institution.

USE OF THIS HANDBOOK

Comparison of the suggestions contained in this handbook with the operational practices of a board should show clearly the differences, and enable responsible persons at the institution to determine whether the things suggested here might be beneficial. That is the desire of the writer and the purpose of the writing.

Bibliography

American Association for Higher Education, Task Force on Faculty Representation and Academic Negotiations, Campus Governance Programs. *Faculty Participation in Academic Governance.* Washington, DC: American Association for Higher Education, 1967.

American Association of University Professors. *Policy Documents and Reports.* Washington, DC: American Association of University Professors, 1977.

Anderson, G. L. *The Evaluation of Academic Administrators; Principles, Processes, and Outcomes.* University Park, PA: Pennsylvania State University, 1975.

Association of Governing Boards of Universities and Colleges, AGB. *Survey of Board Chairmen Opinion.* Washington, DC: Association of Governing Boards of Universities and Colleges, 1973.

Association of Governing Boards of Universities and Colleges, AGB. *Survey of Board Chairmen Opinion.* Washington, DC: Association of Governing Boards of Universities and Colleges, 1974.

Association of Governing Boards of Universities and Colleges and National Association of College and University Business Officers. *Financial Responsibilities of Governing Boards of Colleges and Universities.* Washington, DC: Association of Governing Boards of Universities and Colleges and National Association of College and University Business Officers, 1979.

Baldridge, J. W. *Power and Conflict in the University.* New York: Wiley, 1971.

Bok, D.C. "Reflections on the Ethical Problems of Accepting Gifts: An Open Letter to the Harvard Community." *Harvard University Gazette*, Supplement, 4 May 1979.

Carnegie Commission on Higher Education. *Governance of Higher Education: Six Priority Problems.* New York: McGraw-Hill, 1973.

Corson, J. J. *The Governance of Colleges and Universities.* Revised edition. New York: McGraw-Hill, 1975.

Davis, J. S., and S. A. Batchelor, *The Effective College and University Board: A Report of a National Survey of Trustees and Presidents*. Research Triangle Park, NC: Research Triangle Institute, Center for Educational Research and Evaluation, 1974.

Epstein, L. D. *Governing the University: The Campus and the Public Interest*. San Francisco: Jossey-Bass, 1974.

Hartnett, R. T. *College and University Trustees: Their Backgrounds, Roles, and Educational Attitudes*. Princeton, NJ: Educational Testing Service, 1969.

Healy, R. M., and V. T. Peterson, *"Who Killed These Four Colleges?" AGB Reports* 19:3 (1977): 14-18.

Heilbron, L. H. *The College and University Trustee: A View From the Board Room*. San Francisco: Jossey-Bass, 1973.

Ingram, R. T. "How Can Governing Boards Assure Better Planning?" Paper presented at 12th annual meeting of Society for College and University Planning, Seattle, 17 August 1977.

Jay, A. "How to Run a Meeting." *Harvard Business Review* 54 (1976):43-57.

Lyman, R. W. Remarks made to Stanford University alumni, San Francisco, 7 May 1973.

McGrath, E. J. *Should Students Share the Power?* Philadelphia: Temple University Press, 1970.

Miller, W. F. "How Stanford Plans." *AGB Reports* 20:5 (1978): 26-30.

Morrison, R. S. *Students and Decision Making*. Washington, DC: Public Affairs Press, 1970.

Nason, J. S. *Presidential Search: A Guide to the Process of Selecting and Appointing College and University Presidents*. Washington, DC: Association of Governing Boards of Universities and Colleges, 1979.

Nason, J. W. *The Future of Trusteeship: The Role and Responsibilities of College and University Boards*. Washington, DC: Association of Governing Boards of Universities and Colleges, 1975.

Nason, J. W., and G. P. Wood, "Student-Faculty Trusteeship: A Short Debate." *AGB Reports* 19:2 (1977):12-14.

Nelson, C. A. "Wanted: Strong Trustees for Strong Boards." *Trustee* 31:11 (1978):21-25.

Rauh, M. A. *The Trusteeship of Colleges and Universities*. New York: McGraw-Hill, 1969.

Wriston, Henry. *Academic Procession.*

Zwingle, J. L. *Effective Trusteeship: Guidelines for Board Members*. Washington, DC: Association of Governing Boards of Universities and Colleges, 1979.

Index